I0820111

NAT CARDOZO

ORIGIN

With the collaboration of María José Ferrada on the text

Translated by **IAN FARNES and LAYLA BENITEZ-JAMES**

RED COMET PRESS • BROOKLYN

This book is dedicated to Leo and to my children and my parents for their support and unconditional love, which drives everything I do.

A huge thank-you to my editors, Fernando and Estrella, for their trust and their wonderful work.

To María José Ferrada, for her beautiful words, and to the anthropologists Gabriela Karasik, Carina Gómez, and Ángela Yankillevich, for their crucial involvement in the project.

Above all, I want to dedicate this book to the original peoples of the world, who, with their wisdom, integrity, and persistence, are an example to us all and an endless source of inspiration.

—Nat

Origin

This English edition published in 2025 by Red Comet Press, LLC, Brooklyn, NY

English language edition arranged through Martina Nommel Agencia Literaria, Germany

Library of Congress Control Number: 2024943922
ISBN (HB): 978-1-63655-155-5
ISBN (EBOOK): 978-1-63655-154-8

25 26 27 28 29 TLF 10 9 8 7 6 5 4 3 2 1

First Edition
Manufactured in China using FSC paper
Red Comet Press is distributed by ABRAMS, New York

RedCometPress.com

CONTENTS

INTRODUCTION

The mistake was in thinking the earth belonged to us when the truth is that we belong to the earth.

—Nicanor Parra

There are words that hold within them the complexity of the whole world: "Origin" is one of those words. At our point of origin, all the living beings that now inhabit Earth were stardust. We are made of the remains of stars that died billions of years ago. It is this shared origin that connects us to all other living beings, to nature, and to the multidimensional fabric of the whole universe.

Origin is also the title of this book. A personal journey undertaken over the past ten years, it has been a journey full of questions about our relationship with the planet, where the answers made me turn my attention, again and again, to the people "who have been here since our beginnings," from our shared origin. This is a way of thinking about the Indigenous people of the world, exploring an extensive timeline, from an almost mythical past, that reaches right into our present.

The twenty-two peoples represented in this book are only a small part of the more than five thousand who currently live in the world. They inhabit—and are part of—different ecosystems on five continents, including hostile territories and climates. Some communities, such as the Tuaregs, number more than one million people, and others, such as the Uru Chipaya, number only a couple of thousand. All of them have something in common: Despite many obstacles, they've managed to maintain ways of life where the relationship with nature is based on respect, cohesion, and gratitude.

For Moken children, silence is a sign of respect and a form of communication with animals. The fate of the Inuit is tied to the icy Arctic Ocean. Peoples such as the Ngāti Hau, the Anangu, or the Mbuti have fought for decades for their sacred places, such as rivers, mountains, or forests, to be respected.

They are peoples for whom a sense of community living based on the principle of sharing is of the utmost importance, a sense of solidarity and mutual aid, of avoiding excesses and being thankful for what we get. Indigenous communities take care of nature because they think of it as a living being that they inhabit and that inhabits them, something which is part of who they are. Nature is part of their family: It's their mother, their siblings, their ancestors. A Gitxsan saying explains it perfectly: "Our health depends on how we treat ourselves and upon everything else that exists beneath the sky of this immense place that is our planet." Indigenous peoples, more than 470 million people among them, are also some of the most socially marginalized populations in the world today.

Despite the dispossession of their lands and their rights, the imposition of foreign languages, religions, and customs, most Indigenous communities live in relation to nature in a radically different way from those who only see it as a resource that they can exploit to the point of exhaustion.

This book pays tribute to the Indigenous peoples who have bravely persevered to this day and whose ancestral wisdom has so much to teach us. "The world is a mystery that is discovered little by little," the Bijagós tell us. Through these stories, which condense years of reading and exploration, we will discover how our ability to grow and care for things has a lot to do with listening to the heartbeat of the forest or the mountain, with observing how the wind moves the dunes, and through understanding that singing, dancing, and listening to the old legends is as important as laughter.

Turning our attention to our shared origins implies remembering that everything is connected, understanding that all living beings in this world form a whole and that WE ARE ALL ONE.

Nat Cardozo

!KUNG

Territory: Southern Africa, Kalahari Desert (Botswana, Namibia, and South Africa) and Angolan Tropical Forests
Population: about 50,000 people
Language: !Kung

. . .

The Kalahari Desert is a large red, white, and gray plain. It is a heart from which baobabs spring and through which antelopes, wildebeests, and meerkats run. Their steps, together with ours, follow the rhythm of the oldest song of all. Studies of our DNA show that the !Kung were at the beginnings of everything.

Nomads, hunters, and gatherers follow traces of water and food, and following the paths of our ancestors connects us with an animal awareness. The few objects we have are shared, they belong to all of us. We use them imaginatively and inventively, without clinging to them. The desert has taught us to carry a light load.

Our houses last for a couple of months and, as women, we are in charge of building them with branches. I watch attentively and learn to put the branches together one by one. In the rainy season, the mountain provides us with caves, and we use them as our homes.

Our diet is mostly vegetarian: nuts, berries, and the roots and bulbs that we pick from the deep earth, which give us a long life. Adults teach us to be attentive: There are plants that heal and others that contain poison. The latter help us in hunting animals, which serve as food.

Silence. The hunters, thanks to ancient knowledge, are reading animal tracks and communicating with one another using gestures, a different gesture for each animal. We'll share the food we hunt or gather each day. Those who worked today will rest tomorrow, and so on, every dawn.

Dance and song are as important to my people as laughter. They are what we use to resolve our conflicts. We don't have a writing system, but we do have a rich language containing eighty different types of clicks. "Before time, there was once a lion who did not want to give up his prey," say our grandparents. And we've always, since the very beginning, listened closely.

Honey, insects, ostrich eggs, and, my favorites, the sweet mongongo nuts that fall from the tree and lie everywhere. The arid lands of the Kalahari are teeming with life.

ORANG RIMBA

Territory: Jambi Province, Sumatra, Indonesia
Population: about 3,000 people
Language: Rimba

. . .

Trees that seem to touch the sky surround the wetlands: a blanket of vegetation that helps the earth to breathe. Perched on a branch, the helmeted hornbill shakes its black feathers, while below, a Malaysian tapir searches for fruits and seeds. She's not the only one who's hungry. Hidden in the green, a tiger stalks the Bornean bearded pig. The rhinoceros roars and gigantic carnivorous flowers seem to celebrate the dawn in the forests of Sumatra, our home.

The Orang Rimba, descendants of the Minangkabau, have inhabited this humid land for many years. Following the law of Adat, which says that nature is our queen and teacher, our lives are linked to the trees. In their language of leaves and roots, they tell us that to be born is to bloom, and to die is to wither.

Like everyone else, I'm connected to two trees that protect me. Next to the roots of the first one—a sentubung—my mother buried her placenta, making it my spiritual brother forever. The second—a hardwood senggeris—has given me strength from the first day that the shaman made an ointment from its bark, rubbed it on the crown of my head, and found my name. My trees have always been with me, and everything that happens to them affects me.

Fruits, animals, rivers, and, of course, trees are inhabited by gods. They take different forms and communicate with us through dreams. I recently had a dream where the spirit of an elephant reminded me that its species is sacred and cannot be hunted. I wonder if any other children dreamed that night about the animals we protect, such as the tiger, the orangutan, or the anteater.

As nomads, we travel through the jungle, passing places where someone died or, as we understand it, withered and was left behind. When the deep sadness of death disappears, the forest regenerates its essence. As our proverb says, "Ado rimba ado bungo. Ado bungo ado dewo": "If there is a forest, there will be flowers. If there are flowers, there will be gods."

The earth rests: It's the time of animals and bees, of fish and the river.
We go into the forest in search of life, roots, and shoots, and it awaits us, wherever we go.

INUIT

Territory: Northern Canada, Alaska, and Greenland
Population: about 70,000 people
Language: Inuktitut

. . .

The polar bear plays with her cubs, and a pair of black eyes appear in the middle of the blizzard. It's the white wolf moving along the riverbank in search of salmon. Like us, he knows our icy landscape is full of life: bowhead whales, narwhals, bearded seals, and walruses all live here in the heart of the cold Arctic.

Thousands of years ago, a culture called Thule gave rise to my ancestors. They had to adapt to living in the most inhospitable region on Earth, the tundra, a place where nothing can grow except moss and some wildflowers because of our long winters. But we've learned to love nature. We know that our destiny and the destiny of this ocean of ice are connected.

The caribou, the dogs that drive our sleds, the midnight sun, the glaciers, the weather, everything is endowed with a sacred spirit, called inua, which we must never offend. We express our respect for these protective forces through rites, ceremonies, and magical songs, which are passed down from parent to child. Hunting and fishing are very important for our survival and in our day-to-day lives. We see them as part of a collaborative relationship with animals.

Our grandparents say the animals would be offended and leave if we stopped hunting. At the same time, they also explain something every Inuit must know: Killing animals without reason or hunting more than necessary is a serious crime. If someone commits that crime, they risk the worst punishment: being expelled from our beloved place. I wonder if it would be possible to live without seeing the white of our world. I know I couldn't...

The great spirit of Sedna, protector of all marine animals, teaches us to care for the life that lives in the water: from tiny fish to the immense whale. This is how we maintain harmony between human beings and animals, between land and sea.

While walking along the riverbank during one of our short summers, my father came across this soapstone rock. For days, he watched it and listened to it whisper. Then he knew: Inside the stone was Sedna's spirit! Little by little, through carving and sanding it, he set the spirit free. The carving is a reminder of his teachings.

TUAREG

Territory: desert areas of North Africa (Mali, Algeria, Niger, Burkina Faso, and Libya)
Population: between 1 and 3 million people
Language: Tamasheq

. . .

There was a time when our desert, the Sahara, was a green patch of forest and enormous grasslands, when hunters and gatherers traveled over it. Plants and animals were able to live without fearing the sun, but when the temperatures rose, everything changed. Greens and blues turned ochre, and the ground turned to dust and sand. Even so, there were species that managed to adapt to this desert. It's as beautiful as it is difficult to inhabit. If anyone knows this, it's us, the Tuaregs.

Our story began thousands of years ago, when our ancestors, the Imazighen or "free people," came here, herding their flocks. Since then, wars and conflicts have prevented us from inhabiting any defined territory, but we have a culture and a language that unites us in the form of riddles, proverbs, and animal stories. My favorites are those featuring camels, our loyal friends.

In the evenings, in the Hoggar Mountains, we hear the legend of Tin Hinan, the nomadic queen. It's said that she went on a journey that lasted days and days, along the fiery path of the sand, only following the stars. I wonder if all Tuareg women, strong and wise, are descended from her. That would explain why it's the women who choose where to set up our camp and teach reading and writing, while the men are in charge of going in search of pastures and wells.

We walk to the rhythm of the desert, our king, which has forged our nomadic spirit and taught us to look at the sky as if it were a map. It has also taught us to read the winds and the sand; we can even learn things from their texture and taste! Only sandstorms make us run. In the silence of the desert, I hear my own heartbeat. We have very few possessions, but each and every one of them has enormous value.

We are also called "blue men" or "people of the veil" because we wear an indigo turban that slowly dyes our skin. This fabric can be more than thirty-two feet long. It protects my father from the sand when he's on his way to the market, a journey that could last months.

MOKEN

Territory: Mergui Archipelago (southern Myanmar) and Surin Islands (west coast of Thailand)
Population: between 3,000 and 3,500 people
Language: Moken

. . .

I was born on the turquoise waters of the Indian Ocean, on a houseboat called a kabang. According to an ancient legend, the kabang is like a body that welcomes us. It is a symbol of our nomadic life. Everything happens in the sea. Under the shelter of Lau Gai, the star that never goes away, my brothers and I dive and swim among the coral reefs, home to octopuses, crabs, urchins, and tropical fish.

I really like diving. I learned to swim before I even learned to walk, and my pupils have adapted to the depths of the sea; that's why Moken boys and girls see underwater almost as well as dolphins or seals. They also call us chao ley or the "water people."

My people have always lived between the land and the sea, like turtles. We only live in huts in the monsoon season, when heavy rains and swells force us to take refuge on the islands, sheltered by the forest. We fish with harpoons made of bamboo and, during those four months in the village, we also collect fruits, roots, honey, and wild yams, and repair our kabang.

The elders say that if you take care of your kabang, it will take you wherever you want to go. We build it from the trunk of a single tree, the rakam palm tree, but first we ask permission from the guardian spirit of the tree. If it accepts, we cut the tree down and hollow it out in the forest. Then, on the beach, with very simple tools and some small bonfires, we finish making it. Each kabang is marked by the character of the family that built it.

When the afternoon comes, we gather and sing songs about the old legends that carry the wisdom of our ancestors, such as the legend of laboon, the giant wave that takes the water from the shore and engulfs humans. In our language, there is no word for "desire," because we find food, medicine, and shelter in the sea and the forest. There is no room for the idea of wealth or that they'll be more tomorrow than there is today.

When we're close to a dolphin or a whale, we remain silent as a sign of respect; for us, that silence is a form of communication between two worlds.

ANANGU

Territory: Northern South Australia
Population: between 5,000 and 6,000 people
Languages: Pitjantjatjara, Yankunytjatjara, and Ngaanyatjarra

. . .

In the time of creation, the sun rose in the sky and started to warm the earth. The valleys, the mountains, and the plains came to life just like the kangaroo, the wombat, the koala, the man, and the woman came to life. In the distance, someone sings by the waterhole and picks up a handful of desert sand while talking to the Rainbow Serpent, the sacred spirit who brings rain and storms.

Since time immemorial, the Anangu have inhabited the desert, crowned by Ulurú, the sacred mountain. This immense rock, located in the heart of Australia, connects us with our ancestors, Tjukaritja, who guide us in our relationship with nature and other living beings. They brought rivers, rocks, animals, plants, and human beings to life.

When Ulurú reflects the reddish light of the sunset, my grandfather and other Anangu elders tell the stories of the Tjukurpa, which is the foundation of our culture, beliefs, and ways of life. My friends and I listen, and we find answers to the questions that matter to us: How was the world created, and who created it? Learning these stories, which have never been written, can take many years, and, like my grandfather says, as we grow up, we find new or deeper meanings in them that can guide our lives.

The iwara are the paths that intertwine the sacred places of the Tjukurpa; they are part of a living map that describes a specific path, and each of these places gives evidence of the passage of the ancestral beings that narrate the story of creation. All forms of expression, such as music, songs, dances, and painting, help us to represent Tjukurpa, the story of all stories. Clapping hands or sticks together and singing also marks the rhythm of the inma, our sacred songs and dances.

As Anangu, we paint our bodies with natural dyes. Sitting in a semicircle, we play the didgeridoo, a wind instrument made from the trunk of a eucalyptus tree that has been hollowed out by termites.

BIJAGÓ

Territory: West Africa, archipelago of Bijagós Islands (Guinea-Bissau)
Population: about 20,000 people
Language: Bijagó

. . .

Seen from the sky, the islands look like a drawing surrounded by sand and painted with forest. The aerial roots of the tarrafe mangroves form a fabric under the salt waters, which is a haven for fish, green turtles, mollusks, and crocodiles. I look up, and my eyes find a family of pelicans. I look down, and they stop at the savannah's lake, where the hippo bathes in the bright morning sun.

The Bijagó people are spread across the islands and organized into small villages, which we call tabankas. Legend has it that Nindo created the world on an island he named Orango, where Okanto and Obide, the first woman and the first man, lived. They had four daughters who gave rise to the matrilineal clans that govern our way of life. The Oracuma clan received the land and its ceremonies, as well as the right to carve the statues where the spirits live. Oraga and his family were granted the prairies in all their abundance. Ominka and his family were given the sea and fishing, and finally, the Ogubane clan—to which I belong and inherited from my mother—were given the power of wind and rain.

Certain forests and islands are sacred and untouchable, such as Poliao, the magical island where turtles go to lay their eggs without being disturbed. We cannot hunt or farm them; instead, we get to know them over time, once we overcome the different rites of passage that reveal sacred secrets to us. For us, the world is a mystery that is being discovered little by little. That is why we respect the wisdom of our elders.

When carnival arrives, everything is filled with colors and masks. We move to the rhythm of the drum, representing the personalities and customs of animals. Every moment of life has its dance and every movement a purpose: Ritual dances are paths connecting us to the spirits of the natural world.

The craftsman who made my mask learned his trade from his father, who in turn learned it from his father. Days of seclusion and purification allow us to shape sacred objects. Only I can wear my mask, and it will accompany me throughout my life as well as in my death.

EVENKI

Territory: Eastern Siberia (Russia), northern China, and Mongolia
Population: about 70,000 people
Language: Evenki

The reindeer make their way through the boreal forest. We move with them, among the small rivers and bushes of the Siberian taiga. Along the way, we greet the brown bear, the wolf, and the lynx. We see the sun shining as if it's trying to melt the ice that covers everything.

We have been nomads and reindeer herders for thousands of years. That's why I'm happy when my father tells me that I'm a good rider. Little by little, he can see I'm starting to recognize the signs of the road, despite the snow. We move along routes that only we know, always looking for the best path for our reindeer.

The tents, known in my language as cuoluozi, give us shelter. Fire also helps us survive. My father will thank it by throwing a few drops of vodka, tea, or milk into the flames tonight. Tomorrow, he'll go hunting before the sun rises. Enacting a rite, he'll ask permission from the animal's soul, which is free to accept or refuse the treatment he offers. When I grow up, I'll go with him; I'll know which rivers will be frozen and firm enough to walk on, how to track animals, and where to find lichens and mushrooms to feed the reindeer.

Tonight, the moon is like a giant snowflake peeking out from among the conifers. We look at the immense night and remember how all living beings have a soul called omi. The mountain, the river, the fire, they all have this spirit. By studying the landscape, we can read the messages of Mother Earth, who we call Buga; if we pay close attention, Buga speaks to us.

When night falls, we gather to talk about how the day went and to listen to our ancient stories full of wisdom about the forest. We listen with wide eyes and open ears. One day, when we're the ones in charge of looking for food, these lessons will be our guide: "Once upon a time, there was a man who went out of the camp in search of his reindeer . . . Once upon a time, there was a frozen river that the deer crossed every afternoon . . ."

Generosity is one of Buga's laws, a principle of balance that governs relationships between all living things. If you need my talisman, it's yours. It will protect you as it has protected me.

BRIBRI

Territory: Talamanca mountain range (Costa Rica and Panama)
Population: between 7,000 and 12,000 people
Language: Bribri

In the tropical forest—protected by the guava and banana trees, comfrey, and goosefoot—grow plants that cure illnesses like the ones caused by snake bites. All of us, including me, are sheltered by the great shade of laurels and cedars. Their high branches are home to clay-colored thrushes and toucans that crisscross the morning sky. The trees also feed other animals, such as tapirs, peccaries, and lowland paca, which sniff through the leaf litter in search of fruit.

The first nine Bribri clans were born on the mountain of Suláyöm, from the corn planted by the god Sibö, creator of the universe. All of the birds belong to the Duriwak; all clay pots and urns belong to the Uniwak; all tubers belong to the Tubolwak; the Diwowak own the sun; the yellow dung flies belong to the Kollkiwak; the Bulbulwak own the apiaries; the Sulariwak own the coconut palms; all felines belong to the Usekol mulrë; and the Amazonian motmot belongs to the Tuariwak. The Awapa are traditional doctors to whom we listen with great respect. They speak to us through the suwos (spiritual stories and songs), which hold the wisdom of our people.

Everything in the forest is connected. My grandmother explained this to my mother, and she explained it to me, following an ancient matrilineal thread. We were born from a seed planted by Sibö, which gave us a special talent for growing plants but also the responsibility of care. We learned to plant and farm in a spiral, following the natural wisdom of plant organization, which we call skowak. Skowak teaches us to maintain, nurture, and protect nature. The forest and its trees are sacred to my people. I read its signs, and I can feel its heartbeat. I know if its heart is full of joy or sadness. Everything comes to our ears as if it were the oldest of vibrations. Everything comes to us in the form of stories and songs.

My grandmother says that cocoa, called Tsuru in our language, is the soul of Sibö's wife. She was given the form of this tree so that she could feed her sons and daughters with the fruit from which we make the chocolate drink.

CHEROKEE

Territory: Appalachian Mountains, Oklahoma, and North Carolina (USA)
Population: about 280,000 people; worldwide about 450,000
Language: Cherokee (Tsalagi)

The water cascades from the waterfall, and an eagle pierces the blanket of fog that envelops the Great Smoky Mountains. The moose, otter, groundhog, and squirrel awaken. In a while, they'll begin their journey along the banks of the Mississippi River in search of fruits and seeds. I like to hide behind the oak trees and watch them without them seeing me.

There are seven sacred trees that grow in the prairies. Seven is also the number of clans that the Ani-Yun-Wiya, also known as the Cherokee, belong to. We have seven ceremonies, and there are seven colors to which we associate the universe. For us, there are even seven cardinal points: to the north, the south, the east, and west, we also add the space above, the space below, and the center.

According to our ancestors, the universe is made up of three levels. The upper world, linked to fire, is the domain of the sun: the ancestors who guide us and all that we can foresee. The lower world, related to water, is the place of destructive spirits, the future, and change. Finally, the middle world is the space inhabited by human beings, animals, and plants. Lightning, smoke, and stones also exist; each one, big or small, has its own path, will, intelligence, and sense of perception.

Respecting the Great Spirit means maintaining the balance between different the forces that cooperate in harmony: man and woman; hunting and harvesting; human beings and animals. We also have to maintain the balance inside of us.

I teach my little brother the principle of balance that we call tohi: We don't take what we want from nature, just what we need. This way of understanding life and the cosmos, as a single universal energy, forges a great sense of justice, forgiveness, and love among us.

The sacred fire cannot be extinguished with water. Each element belongs to a domain. Our balance depends on avoiding contamination between one domain and another, so we stay healthy and have good harvests.

MOSUO

Territory: Southwest China, on the shores of Lake Lugu (between Yunnan and Sichuan provinces)
Population: about 40,000 people
Language: Na (Tibetan-Burmese language group)

. . .

In a corner of the Himalayas, Ge Mu, the goddess of the mountain, shed tears of love, and Lugu Lake was born. Every morning, we women gather on its shore to pray. Did you know that we only go into it on wooden boats? We don't want to contaminate the crystal-clear water. We love it, and it loves us. We call it the Mosuo, or the Na, in our language.

Our territory, known as the kingdom of women, is organized around matriarchs who lead our community. For a long time, my house has provided shelter to a great family: my mother, my maternal aunts and uncles, my grandmother, my great-grandmother, my great-great-grandmother . . . and to me, one more bud on their powerful tree.

They teach me many things. For example, in our culture, marriage is based on affection, so women and men do not necessarily live under the same roof, and they take care of raising children together only if they agree to.

Women do farm and household chores. Men, on the other hand, make religious and political decisions. Then, the matriarch, who is not always the oldest woman but the wisest, decides on specific tasks according to our strengths and abilities.

The stories and traditions of our people are passed down orally with the assistance of Daba priests. Daba is the native religion of the Mosuo and says that everything has a soul. This influences the way we look at the world.

Tomorrow, I have a very important birthday: I'll be thirteen. I'll have my own room. After the skirt ceremony, I'll be able to wear my traditional dress for the first time. I will also pay my respects to my dog. According to a very old legend, dogs used to live for a long time, but they decided to exchange their long life with humans in an act of generosity. Since then, they have been venerated by the whole community.

Upon reaching this important moment, thirteen-year-old boys and girls perform a rite that consists of putting one foot on a dry cedar and the other on a sack of rice. We ask that abundance and prosperity accompany us for the rest of our lives.

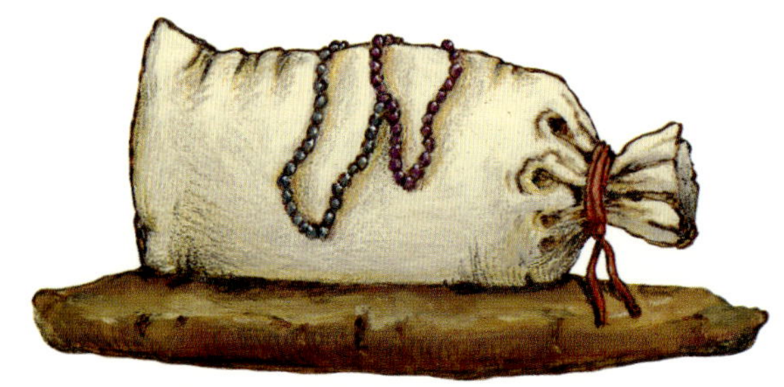

URU CHIPAYA

Territory: Santa Ana de Chipaya, Department of Oruro, Western Bolivia
Population: about 2,000 people
Language: Chipaya

. . .

Andean flamingos called pariwanas dye the sky pink between the Payachatas' snow-capped peaks and the Andes Mountains. I wave my hat in greeting from this mirror of the sky, an aquamarine salt flat known as Salar de Coipasa, guarded by huge cacti. If your eyes get used to the desert's harsh brightness—as ours have after thousands of years of living in this place—you'll be able to clearly distinguish the armadillos, which we call quirquinchos, partridges, and lizards moving across the wetlands.

In the beginning of everything, they say only the moon shone alone in the sky. It was the Chullpas, the first inhabitants, who, looking at the sky, noticed the arrival of the sun, which came to burn everything. Even so, they stayed, and only one man and one woman survived, hidden in the waters of the Lauca River. This is how the Urus Chipayas or Qnas Soñi were born, the "people of the water."

We've learned to adapt to nature and its difficulties: floods, droughts, hail, snowfall, lightning, and hurricanes. We were able to achieve all this with the wisdom and creativity that allows us to move the dunes from their place, to redirect the watercourses, and take advantage of the winds from each of the four cardinal points. Under the guidance of the Jilakata who runs our community, we wash the salty soil and prepare it for quinoa and cañihua seeds.

Boys and girls also work together to feed the community, taking charge of identifying edible eggs. The secret, as my older brother taught me, is to scratch them gently and hold them up to the light. Mothers and fathers appreciate these gifts, which we proudly carry in our hands as if they were the fruits of heaven.

We ask permission from Pachamama and the water spirits—Quta mama and Quta papa—to build our adobe houses and help us navigate. Also, for permission to harvest totora roots and the fruits of aquatic plants that have served as our food for centuries.

TZ'UTUJIL

Territory: Sololá (Guatemala)
Population: about 106,000 people
Language: Tz'utujil

. . .

Hummingbirds flit, and parrots and white herons fly around the grasslands growing on the edge of Lake Atitlán. With their colors and songs, they celebrate the existence of the deep, blue waters. At this height, much higher than sea level, three giants are in charge of guarding them. They are the San Pedro, Tolimán, and Atitlán volcanoes. Yes, the latter shares the name with the lake, just as I share my days with all the life that comes through here. In this moment, a kingfisher appears. Will he visit the great quetzal's house? With his long, brightly colored tail, the quetzal is the god of the air.

On the slopes of the San Pedro volcano is the territory inhabited by the Tz'utujils, known as Tz'ikinajaa or "lord of the birds." Here, with the help of our grandparents, we learn a secret language: If clouds surround the volcano, a hurricane rain is coming, and if a woodpecker sings in our left ear, it's a sign that we must hold on to hope. If, on the other hand, he sings in our right ear, he's warning us of danger. My favorite is the hummingbird's message that is responsible for bringing the good thoughts other people have for us. Today, one came to visit. Could it be that my friend is thinking of me?

The conversation with nature continues in our clothes. My mother is in charge of weaving the fabric of the güipil using her loom, while my aunt and I are in charge of dyeing the skirt and its "cut." When everything is ready, my father will be in charge of drawing the birds, which we women will embroider with colored threads. In ceremonies, we adorn ourselves with a red ribbon, called tocoyal or xq'op. We wind the tocoyal around our heads twenty times for the twenty days in the Mayan calendar. The red ribbon is embroidered with colorful scenes that narrate our traditions; it represents the continuity of life.

The quetzal, the hummingbird, and the tanager appear flying across the chest of my güipil.
I imagine that the lake, the volcanoes, and the birds of the sky all agree:
Our clothing is beautiful!

NGĀTI HAU

Territories: North Island (New Zealand)
Population: about 42,300 people
Language: Māori

. . .

"Ko au te awa, ko te awa ko au." "I am the river, the river is me." I say it first, and my younger sister repeats it, as if it were an echo. We are tied to the Whanganui river. We feel it every time we gaze into its currents or enter it—our hearts beat to the rhythm of its waters. Whanganui takes its strength from the volcanoes, providing us with its spirit and care. Its health is ours; its well-being too.

Water surrounds us and forms part of the Māori creation story—we are called the Tangata Whenua in our own language, "people of the island." They say, hundreds of years ago, seven boats led by our ancestors crossed the blue back of the Pacific Ocean and arrived at these islands: Aotearoa—the "land of the great white cloud."

A tribe, or iwi, arrived at each one. My sister, who loves birds, asks me if those men and women might have seen the kakapo parrot, the weka, and the kiwi when they found land. The truth is, I don't know. Instead, I tell her that there was a time when the birds she names flew, but since they had no predators, they stopped flying. It happened a long time ago . . .

We are part of a network of relationships connecting everything—the animals, plants, rocks, volcanoes, and the Whanganui. We are also connected to the kauri, our beloved tree; the white-headed dolphin; and the tuatara, a reptile. To us, no life is superior to another.

Who we are and all that is sacred to us is reflected in many ways in our culture: painting, weaving, carving, and also in the tattoos we call Tā moko, which include symbols of our beliefs and sacred nature, such as the kuri fern, whose spiral represents the path of life.

We receive tattoos as part of our rite of passage into adulthood. They tell the story every Ngāti Hau carries inside, that the tattoo artist, a sacred person in our community, masterfully takes care of releasing from within us.

The tattoos on the left side of my face are connected to my father's story, and the ones on my right side connect to my mother's. The tattoos' main lines, called manawa or "heart," represent the journey of my existence. And just as no two lives are the same, there are no two Ngāti Hau tattooed in the same way.

WAYUU

Territory: Guajira Peninsula (between the extreme northeast of Colombia and the extreme northwest of Venezuela)
Population: about 700,000 people
Language: Wayuunaiki

. . .

In the story of "Woummainpa," the ancestral land of the Guajira, the river joins the sea like a transparent ribbon, leaving space for the mangroves. If you follow the weave of the fabric, you can see how the desert lives alongside blue shores—how the hawksbill turtle, the mangrove boa, and the yellow parrot are part of the thread that holds everything together.

Legend has it that the great-grandmother Sawai Piushii (known as the deep darkness of the night) and the great-grandfather Araliatü'ü-Warattuy (known as the clarity of the sky) were the first inhabitants of this place. Sawai Piushii made the sun and the moon. Araliatü'ü-Warattuy made the land and the sea. Then it was the plants' and animals' turn. The first Wayuu being was transformed from the animals, which contained all the elements of the cosmos. In remembrance of this sacred origin, we organize ourselves into clans, each linked to an animal or totem.

When it's time, the elders tell us stories that help us understand how everything came into being. Nothing is written on paper, but instead it's written on our traditional fabrics and kanaas: Their threads, colors, and shapes hold myths and legends only we know how to decipher.

While the men in my family weave sandals, hats, and even roofs for houses with plant fiber, the women use their looms to make hammocks, girdles, and fishing nets, and everyone helps with embroidery. At the beginning of puberty or paülujutu'u, I will have enough knowledge to start learning the craft of weaving.

Grandma says that, with the guidance of the spider spirit Wale'kerü, I'll one day be able to spin and twist thread as well as she and my mother can. I'm waiting for that moment to come as I watch the stitches that unite earth and sky. I am grateful.

My sister focuses on the precise and agile movement of her hands, which, according to our mythology, was taught to the first woman by Wale'kerü. We've been weaving since ancient times to help us remember how we are part of a community.
The material expands and grows in a spiral, like life.

Q'ERO

Territory: East of the province of Paucartambo, Cuzco (Peru)
Population: about 2,000 people
Language: Quechua

. . .

In the central area of the Andes Mountains, large glacial lagoons touch the sky and become a haven for birds, such as the huachua goose. This wild and cold landscape, where the shadow of the condor is projected onto icy mountains, has welcomed us for more than six thousand years. Here bunches of ichu grow, the main food of alpacas and llamas, animals so important to us that they even have their own song.

Our people are the descendants of the Incas and heirs to Andean culture. From my ancestors, we learned that all things—mountains, plants, waterfalls, hummingbirds, and pumas—form one big family. In the Quechua language we call life Sumac Kawsay, "good living," and we understand it as a process in harmony and balance with Pachamama, our Mother Earth.

At the highest plateaus, known as puna, we herd the alpacas and llamas that are essential for our survival, just as our ancestors did. In the Quichua, or central valley, we grow potatoes, which we harvest in as many different varieties as we have ways of cooking them. It is also a place for ceremonies, carnivals, and communal gatherings. Farther down, in the yunga, or valley, we grow corn, squash, and yacon.

Today is sunny, and my sisters and I imitate women who weave with colored threads, sitting on the floor. With wool from alpacas and llamas, we create fabrics whose colors and designs express our way of understanding the world. They describe harvest cycles or portray our myths. Each fabric is like a painting that tells a story. Before knitting, my mother asks permission from the apus, the spirits of the mountains and animals. She sings in a way that unites us to Pachamama, the universe that generates life.

After each harvest, we dig a hole for Pachamama, offer her the best harvested food, thank her, and serve her those offerings. This ceremony is an act of reciprocity that we call ayni, based on the principle of universal balance that governs Andean life.

SÁMI

Territory: Northern Europe (Norway, Sweden, and Finland) and Kola Peninsula (Russia)
Population: about 80,000 people
Language: Sami

. . .

Legend has it that a small fox roamed the skies above the Arctic Circle. He quickly went from one corner to another at night, playing with the stars he found in his path. As he ran around, he slammed his tail against the snow, leaving behind a river of colored sparks that spread and flew overhead. This is how the northern lights that dance upon the frozen earth were born.

Out in the sky on clear nights like this, you'll see the "lights that can be heard" or guovssahas. My family and I remain sheltered from the figures of the luminous dance of the northern lights. The elders say exposing ourselves to them does not bode well. What do the lynx, musk ox, snowy owl, or lemming do? Do they come out of hiding to greet the green light?

For thousands of years, we've herded reindeer on these cold roads. Lichens, crowberries, and blueberries have managed to adapt to the soil. Fungi and algae grow here too, providing food for animals. As we enter the coniferous forest, we are accompanied by the gods who are all around us.

The weight of snowflakes has once again beaten the branches of the birch tree. White is once again lost in white, in a cycle that marks the winter we know so well. It's a landscape that contrasts with the vibrant colors of our clothing. The gátki—that's what we call our special costume—is made with great care and attention by a member of the family or someone else who is close to us.

Tiny beads, colored patches, and pewter wire thread create drawings that reveal many things. For instance, our land of origin, the family we belong to, and even whether we are married or single. They are symbols telling our story, and we wear them with pride and joy.

MBUTI

Territories: Central Africa, Ituri Forest (Northwestern Democratic Republic of the Congo)
Population: about 40,000 people
Language: Mbuti

. . .

Threads of light filter through the branches of immense teak and cedar trees. If you pay attention, you can feel the elephant's footsteps through the soles of your feet as they make the ground tremble. In the trees, you can hear them making a ruckus. The manatee, the hippopotamus, and the crocodile are also moving, following the rhythm of the water. The Ituri Forest is our home.

I wonder if the birds call the forest Mother and Father in their language, like we do. If they sing to those parents as well. To talk to the forest, we sing. To thank it for its generosity, we sing. When we have problems, like an invasion of ants or a sick child, we also sing very loudly to wake the sleeping forest.

The Mbuti respect the law of the forest. Jengi, its spirit, tells us there are animals we can hunt for food, like the mokumbi, or Gambian rat, and others, like the nginiso, the great gorilla, that are prohibited. We know which plants will feed us and which will heal our spirit. They are all essential.

Near here are the swampy forests, dark areas where the sun can't reach. The lianas block our path, as if they were a fabric covering everything. However, plants also clean the air and protect life in the wetlands.

When a Mbuti comes into the world, his mother creates a song for him, and his father is charged with looking for tree bark that will become cloth after being soaked and crushed. Mixing the pigment from roots, fruits, and leaves with charcoal, the women decorate this bark cloth. Drawing with their fingers or with fine branches, they decorate it with the sounds of insects or an image of the sun. This clothing is like the forest, like a mother's womb; it protects me through different stages of life.

The fabric that will wrap my brother mixes drawings and empty spaces. We call this emptiness ekimi or the "silence of the forest," and we associate it with tranquility. The forest is never silent. My mother explained this to me, and I'll explain it to my brother: Its voice sustains us.

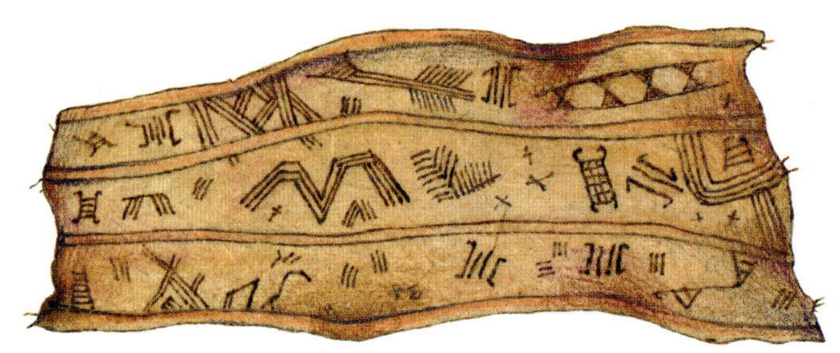

JUCHITECA

Territory: Juchitán, Isthmus of Tehuantepec (Mexico)
Population: about 86,000 people
Language: Didxazá (Zapotec)

. . .

We live in the "land of flowers," on a narrow strip of earth between two great oceans. We are the Juchiteca people. I wonder if the harpy eagle and the king vulture confuse us women with walking flowers when they look down and see our colorful huipils, or if the ocelot and the peccary, who share this tropical and mountainous land with us, think our heads are blooming when they see our hairstyles.

Our roots are located in the heights of Cerro del Jaguar, where the "people of the clouds" or the Zapotecs settled. The name of our town, Juchitán, comes from Guie'xhuuba, which is also known as "jasmine of the Isthmus" or "powerful flower of the underworld." The elders say that this treasure, white and perfumed, used to be given as a gift to the allied peoples and that, when we refused to give it to Moctezuma II, a war broke out. In the end they managed to take the flower, but it withered and died!

The women of my family run the business of taking things to market. They make food such as iguana stew, fresh red snapper, tortilla chips, and sweet corn tamales, and take our typical handicrafts with them: huaraches, xicalpestles, and embroidered gala dresses. We display these things in the velas, the main festivals, that are celebrated with a joyful parade of floats adorned with flowers, especially in May.

We use flowers both to celebrate life and to celebrate death. As well as wearing them as headdresses and embroidering them onto our garments, we embellish altars with flowers in both the temple and in the heart of our homes. At the end of each October, the dead cross a portal with four corners—there are four cardinal points, four jaguars that sustain the world—and, after nourishing themselves with our offering of fruits and bread, they return to their world along a path that we decorate with candles, copal, and marigold petals. I wonder if our beloved flowers will also grow in that place, which only the dead can know.

In the ritual, which we call biyé, we venerate those who have departed, as well as Bisilú, god of death, and Guzanado, god of life. You can also see the jaguar is there, and he presides over two very important tasks: protecting nature and accompanying souls.

GITXSAN

Territories: Northwest British Columbia (Canada)
Population: about 5,600 people
Language: Gitxsan

. . .

The sun shines on the high glacier-covered mountains of Skeena country. Sockeye salmon swim upstream with all their might to lay their eggs. On their long journey, some of them will be eaten by the Kermode bear, which we also call the spirit bear.

Maples, stoats, and wolves lurk stealthily among the ancient red cedars. They surround the plants, mosses, and fungi marking the path of the ancient forest that we Gitxsan, or "people of the river mist," have inhabited for thousands of years.

We know the secret of the vegetation growing in the rain, and in case of illness, we turn to the bark of trees and shrubs. Plants can heal and be powerful protective amulets, but just as important as knowing their properties is the attitude with which they are collected and used. The forest has taught us they have their own power to heal us or keep us healthy. And as my mother says: "Health is the result of the care with which we treat ourselves and everything that grows under the sky of this immense place."

We organize ourselves into four clans, Lax Seel (Frog), Lax Gibuu (Wolf), Lax Skiik (Eagle), and Gisghaast (Fire Grass), each with their own territories and fishing grounds. The clans are divided into groups of houses—known as wilp—made up of one or more families, led by a chief, chosen from among us, who has the help of the wise elders.

Today, when evening falls, we'll go out to look for the red cedar with which to make the totem for our wilp. We choose it according to its personality, and we will perform a ceremony for it as a sign of respect and gratitude. This time, I'll also help carve it. I imagine it will be a totem that can be seen from far away, a beautiful totem.

We are almost done. All that remains is to carve the eagle, which is the emblem of our wilp. By putting the totem in front of our house, facing the sea, those who come from the coast will know my family and I live here. In the past, when we traveled by water, that was how we identified ourselves.

DONGRIA KONDH

Territory: State of Odisha (Eastern India)
Population: about 8,000 people
Language: Kui

. . .

With their roots, the trees embrace the Niyamgiri hill range, our beloved home, and much more than that, they embrace our soul. The Malabar giant squirrel, the golden spectacled tegu, and the sloth worship them with every step. Will the water of the stream dance in celebration of their existence?

All of us—living beings and places—have a jela, or "soul," that comes from the mother goddess. We give thanks to the god Niyam Raja, provider and guardian of the forests, and Dharani Penu, goddess of the earth. They have helped us in our task: to protect the mountain and everything that lives on it.

Although our name comes from "donger," which means "hill land," we prefer to be called jharnia or "protectors of the streams." My siblings and I listen to the water singing while we look at the flowers and herbs, which serve as medicine, sprouting near the shore.

It's not just the stream that sings. Those voices that can be heard in the distance, accompanied by drums, scare away any elephants, monkeys, and wild boars that might come near. They know we grow delicious fruits and vegetables.

I could join in the singing, but I need to go home quickly today. It's a special day: For the first time, I'll sleep with the other girls in a shared room called Daa Sala. With the guidance of the elders, we sing, dance, and share myths, legends, and proverbs about sacred femininity. The boys also have a room to share. And they share their stories.

Look! The men and women are covered in tattoos, earrings, necklaces, and bracelets. Some of these ornaments have been with me since my childhood. I look at their reflection in the river. And if I run, with the help of the wind, I hear them tinkling.

Among the old priestesses, whom I lose sight of behind the hill, are my two grandmothers. They head toward the neighboring village to perform the ritual of searching for the ancient millet seeds. They say they are stars hidden within the earth, true treasures.

YANOMAMI

Territory: Southern Venezuela and northern Brazil
Population: between 36,000 and 45,000 people
Language: Yanomami

. . .

One of the women breastfeeds her child as well as a wild boar that has been orphaned. Who knows if he'll want to play with me and the others when he grows up. We'll climb the walnut tree and visit the scarlet macaw, which will give us ceiba seeds and maybe even teach us to fly. Little wild boar, if you are part of the jungle, you are our brother.

And now I'll leave quietly, following even smaller sisters: bees. I saw them a while ago, there, among the orchids. The Yanomami know more than fifty different types of bees and use their honey as food or medicine. Urihi, the "jungle earth," the Amazon, is generous with everyone who lives in this place.

We take care of our mother forest and all the beings that live here with the guidance of Omawë, creator god of the Yanomami. Our nomadic community lives in a large shabono of four hundred people; each family has its own small plot with hammocks to sleep in and a fire to cook on. The center of the shabono is communal and used for meetings where decisions are made by consensus. The jungle teaches us that to maintain interdependence, we are all important: the bee, the little wild boar, and me.

The wind, which whistles between the climbing plants, is always ready to listen to us. I tell it about the trip we'll all make in search of new places to grow bananas, yams, and taros. We'll feed ourselves with what we harvest as well as with spiders, frogs, termites, or the peccaries and tapirs the hunters share with one another, respecting their ancient custom never to eat the meat from their own kill.

And now to walk back home without making a sound. Will the wild boar dream in its sleep? Will the wind know what it dreams about?

We call our body paint Onimou. We pass on messages and identify ourselves with it when we leave the shabono. The red pigment comes from the seed of the annatto and the black pigment from the fruit of the genip tree, which men use when they defend our land. Purple, blue, white: Each color and each shape has a reason and motif.

SAMI
INUIT
GITXSAN
CHEROKEE
TUAREG
WAYUU
BIJAGÓ
YANOMAMI
JUCHITECA
BRIBRI
TZ'UTUJIL
MBUTI
!KUNG
Q'ERO
URU
CHIPAYA

LANDS AND TERRITORIES

To occupy a territory, a piece of our beautiful planet, is not the same thing as inhabiting it. For the Evenkis, for example, to live means to walk the roads that lead from one place to another. From this perspective, we should view any map as a set of interlocking paths.

Indigenous peoples inhabit a quarter of the world, nearly 15 million square miles (of the almost 57 million that make up Earth's land surface) and are the custodians of eighty percent of Earth's biodiversity.

Although they differ greatly in customs and cultures, land and water—fundamental resources of subsistence—all these peoples have a sacred dimension that consumerist societies ignore because they want to exploit the natural resources of these territories for money. Indigenous people choose instead to live in a place in a way that doesn't affect the fate of those other beings who inhabit it or cause the environmental degradation that exploitation produces.

There is a long history of resistance movements and conflict between native peoples and those with powerful exploitative interests. It is also a struggle that implicates the defense of their own languages. Although Indigenous peoples represent five percent of the world's population, they speak more than four thousand languages. However, according to UN estimates, one falls out of use every two weeks.

A territory can sustain a way of life and a language, as well as customs and cultural identity. It can intertwine past, present, and future. A language sustains centuries of history, legends, and knowledge that is transmitted from generation to generation and, with it, ancient information about the sustainable management of the environment, about the survival of our planet.

LEARN MORE, UNDERSTAND MORE

History and Territories

In 1830, the United States Congress passed the Indian Removal Act, which, while dictating "voluntary exile," became a tool to dispossess Native Americans from their territories. The forced migration, known as the Trail of Tears, resulted in widespread suffering and the death of about four thousand **Cherokees**.

During the process of decolonization of the African continent, which began in the mid-nineteenth century, the **Tuareg** were divided among the new borders that were created due to the formation of national states. However, they never felt part of the Malian, Niger, Burkinabe, or Algerian nation and became political refugees within their own borders.

The rainforests of Sumatra, in Indonesia, are home to the **Orang Rimba**, but their religion and nomadic way of life are not recognized by the state. As their forests are destroyed to make way for palm oil plantations, they must move to cities where they are forced to change their beliefs and customs so as not to be abused or mistreated.

In the sixteenth century, the **Mbuti** were taken as slaves to European courts, where they acted as jesters. Their living conditions are still appalling in the twenty-first century because they are not only prohibited from their traditional hunting practices but also expelled from their forests so that their natural resources can be exploited.

Threats and Resistance

The **Sámi** are currently fighting against a wind farm built on the Fosen Peninsula, north of Oslo, which has destroyed their ancestral migration route. Even though the Supreme Court of Norway ruled the installation violates the rights of reindeer herders to develop their culture, the wind farm is still in operation.

A vast expanse of hills and valleys in eastern India form the Niyamgiri mountain range, sacred to the **Dongria Kondh**. The area, rich in bauxite, is the scene of a conflict between Indigenous people and the British company Vedanta Resources Limited, owner of a refinery that causes pollution. The Dongria Kondh eventually won the trial, which barred the company from opening a mine.

In 2017, the **Anangu** managed to ban people from climbing to the summit of Ulurú, a sacred place. The measure took place within the context of a struggle for the recovery of lands that were taken from them during the British invasion in 1770, which also brought epidemics and deaths. Within a span of just a hundred years, the Australian Aborigines have gone from one million to sixty thousand people.

The **!Kung**, like other peoples of the area, have inhabited the Kalahari Desert in southern Africa for more than twenty thousand years. Between 1997 and 2005, after years of harassment, the Gana and Gwi tribes were evicted from the Kalahari Game Reserve and forcibly transferred to resettlement camps, which they describe as "places of death."

The **Q'ero** nation, declared by Peruvians as part of the Cultural Heritage of the Nation, fears for the Andean culture it has largely managed to preserve for centuries. They explain the arrival of mining companies in their territory will contaminate and forever alter their way of life until it also destroys knowledge and traditions that date back to the Inca period.

Environmental Degradation

For more than three decades, Canada's north has been experiencing drastic climatic changes that have reduced Indigenous peoples' access to the natural resources of their traditional environments. This has not only meant a decrease in livelihoods but also had an impact on the cultural practices and health of the Inuit.

The **Wayuu** are suffering the consequences of rising temperatures and reduced rainfall, related to the El Niño phenomenon. In addition to damaging crops, its effects make it difficult to care for the livestock they depend on for survival. As one of their sayings goes: "The Pereskia guamacho can only be fertilized with strong sun and copious rains."

Artists of **Tz'utujil** origin protested against the contamination of Lake Atitlán in a performance in 2022 in Guatemala City. As part of the protests, there were women with canes on their heads carrying plastic waste and garbage instead of fruits and flowers. Men carried soda bottles and old shoes in their nets. Since 2016, a law has prohibited the use of plastics in San Pedro La Laguna.

The waters of the Lauca River irrigate quinoa, potato, and cañihua crops. The **Urus** depend on them for the expansion of their planting areas. But they are becoming scarcer every day. Climate change is compounded by a network of canals that, since 1961, have diverted the course of the river, leaving only ten percent of its total flow in Bolivian territory.

The **Yanomami** suffered a very serious health and food crisis in 2019 due to the invasion of their territory by illegal miners, which was supported by the former Brazilian President Jair Bolsonaro. The so-called "gold rush in the Amazon" took place in the Indigenous reserve over which the community has legal authority. The exploitation of thirty-three percent of the reserve's surface area—some 8 million acres—will make the irreparable damage, described as a genocide, even more profound.

Social Organization and Ancestral Knowledge

In the **Bijagó** community, priestesses—baloberras—are in charge of transmitting the wisdom of the ancestors in a rite that initiates women into the adult world. They also inherit the clan in a line that passes from mothers to daughters.

From an ethnographic point of view, the **Mosuo** are known for their unique model of forming partnerships and reproducing, known as "itinerant marriage." Relationships are open, they don't live together under the same roof, and babies are raised with the mothers' family. This bond and its various traditions are under threat from economic reforms and globalization, in particular from the increase in tourism.

For generations, the **Moken** have told one another the stories of Laboon, the "wave that swallows people." Thanks to this, in 2004, when they saw that the sea was receding, they understood that it was a tsunami. They fled to the high ground, along with the tourists who followed them, saving them from adding to the 230,000 victims killed by the catastrophe on the coasts of the Indian Ocean.

After fifteen years of hard work, the **Evenki** people compiled and produced the Evenki Atlas (2019) and made it available to everyone. It is the first online cultural atlas of Indigenous knowledge whose objective is to preserve the customs, language, and information that the Evenki believe to be valuable to their community.

The **Juchiteca** economic system is run by women. Its priorities are the feeding and care of children and the elderly. They hold collective banquets because, as they say, "no one is left hungry in Juchitán."

20
62
8
+42,01
-80,310
2
19
74
58142
579
-03
20
4
4
6
6
2
092
9
05
7
1
101
4
01 1 10
625 0
+0,1005
84
3,91062

FROM WHERE YOU ARE . . .

Perhaps you can see chimneys that seem to touch the sky and cover the clouds with blankets of smoke. I hope you hear birds. Is there one perched on the branch of the tree that reaches toward your window?

As you read this, it's possible for an infinite snake of cars to slide across the asphalt of the street without pause. Cities can be like jungles, where sirens roar and luminous advertisements of things like smiling chickens are all around you. Bright flashes and loud noise cover the silence. And in your hand, maybe you hold a digital totem that connects you with everyone, all the time . . . but which doesn't protect you.

I don't really know what you look like or the landscape that is reflected in your face: countryside or city, north or south. But you should know that you are unique, different, and important. Your voice and your decisions are too. You are part of this world, and the world is part of you. We all inhabit a landscape, our lives are interwoven with the stone, the ant, and the river. Recognizing this link expands our horizons: That is the greatest of our achievements.

Earth is alive. Self-respect also involves respecting what surrounds us: nature, the ecosystem, the atmosphere, the earth, our resources, and other human beings. Maybe from where you are you can feel that you are part of this community. This also makes us responsible: How much might we grow through understanding that there are other ways to live? Perhaps it is time to remember that nature lives inside each of us, and that we all come from the same ORIGIN.

NAT CARDOZO

Nat is an illustrator and workshop facilitator specializing in editorial illustration. She was born in France, to Uruguayan political refugees. She graduated from the J. Serra i Abella School in Barcelona, Spain. She now lives near Montevideo, Uruguay, where she works as a freelance artist. She has participated in various exhibitions in Uruguay, Mexico, Spain, and Argentina. Nat Cardozo has won multiple awards for children's book illustration. Visit her at nat.cardozo.com.

This project was supervised by a team of anthropologists from the Center for Contemporary Studies at the Southern Andean University, National University of Jujuy, including CONICET* researchers, Dr. Garbriel A. Karasik, Carina Gómez, and Ángela Yankillevich.

*National Scientific and Technical Research Council–Argentina

The stories in this book are inspired by direct testimonies and data obtained from various documentary sources.

At the QR code you will find links to references—including podcasts, blogs, documentary proposals, films, and articles—for anyone who might want to learn more about indigenous peoples and the issues raised in *Origin*.

www.redcometpress.com/originreferences